50 Low-Sodium Meal Recipes

By: Kelly Johnson

Table of Contents

- Grilled Lemon Herb Chicken
- Quinoa and Black Bean Salad
- Baked Salmon with Asparagus
- Zucchini Noodles with Pesto
- Stuffed Bell Peppers
- Vegetable Stir-Fry
- Brown Rice and Vegetable Pilaf
- Roasted Chickpeas and Sweet Potatoes
- Spinach and Mushroom Omelet
- Turkey and Spinach Meatballs
- Baked Tilapia with Lemon and Dill
- Cauliflower Rice Stir-Fry
- Greek Yogurt Chicken Salad
- Vegetable Lentil Soup
- Cabbage and Carrot Slaw
- Chickpea Salad with Cucumber and Tomato
- Grilled Vegetable Skewers
- Quinoa-Stuffed Eggplant
- Chicken and Vegetable Stir-Fry
- Baked Sweet Potatoes with Black Beans
- Veggie-Packed Frittata
- Broccoli and Cauliflower Salad
- Turkey and Vegetable Lettuce Wraps
- Roasted Beet and Arugula Salad
- Sautéed Kale with Garlic
- Mediterranean Couscous Salad
- Stuffed Zucchini Boats
- Lentil and Vegetable Stew
- Oven-Baked Chicken with Herbs
- Fresh Tomato and Basil Pasta
- Grilled Shrimp Tacos with Cabbage Slaw
- Eggplant Parmesan (Low-Sodium)
- Roasted Vegetable Medley
- Wild Rice and Cranberry Salad
- Spaghetti Squash with Marinara

- Chicken Quinoa Bowl
- Asian Cabbage Salad
- Lemon Garlic Shrimp and Broccoli
- Baked Portobello Mushrooms
- Avocado and Tomato Salad
- Vegetable and Bean Chili
- Savory Oatmeal with Spinach
- Grilled Turkey Burgers
- Roasted Brussels Sprouts with Almonds
- Sweet Potato and Black Bean Tacos
- Ratatouille
- Butternut Squash Soup
- Thai Coconut Curry with Vegetables
- Spinach and Feta Stuffed Chicken Breast
- Brown Rice Sushi Rolls

Grilled Lemon Herb Chicken

Ingredients:

- 4 chicken breasts
- 1/4 cup olive oil
- Juice of 2 lemons
- 2 cloves garlic, minced
- 1 tsp dried oregano
- 1 tsp dried thyme
- Salt and pepper to taste

Instructions:

In a bowl, whisk together olive oil, lemon juice, garlic, oregano, thyme, salt, and pepper. Add the chicken breasts and marinate for at least 30 minutes. Preheat the grill to medium-high heat and grill the chicken for 6-7 minutes per side, or until fully cooked. Let rest for a few minutes before slicing and serving.

Quinoa and Black Bean Salad

Ingredients:

- 1 cup quinoa, rinsed
- 2 cups water
- 1 can (15 oz) black beans, rinsed and drained
- 1 red bell pepper, diced
- 1/2 cup corn (fresh or canned)
- 1/4 cup cilantro, chopped
- Juice of 1 lime
- 2 tbsp olive oil
- Salt and pepper to taste

Instructions:

In a pot, bring water to a boil, add quinoa, and reduce to a simmer. Cover and cook for about 15 minutes until water is absorbed. In a large bowl, combine the cooked quinoa, black beans, bell pepper, corn, cilantro, lime juice, olive oil, salt, and pepper. Toss to combine and serve chilled or at room temperature.

Baked Salmon with Asparagus

Ingredients:

- 4 salmon fillets
- 1 bunch asparagus, trimmed
- 2 tbsp olive oil
- 1 lemon, sliced
- Salt and pepper to taste
- 1 tsp garlic powder

Instructions:

Preheat the oven to 400°F (200°C). Arrange the salmon and asparagus on a baking sheet. Drizzle with olive oil, and sprinkle with salt, pepper, and garlic powder. Place lemon slices on top of the salmon. Bake for 15-20 minutes, or until the salmon is cooked through and flakes easily with a fork. Serve warm.

Zucchini Noodles with Pesto

Ingredients:

- 4 medium zucchinis
- 1/2 cup basil pesto
- 1 tbsp olive oil
- Salt and pepper to taste
- Cherry tomatoes, halved (optional)

Instructions:

Using a spiralizer, create zucchini noodles. Heat olive oil in a skillet over medium heat and add the zucchini noodles. Sauté for about 2-3 minutes until slightly softened. Remove from heat, and stir in the pesto. Season with salt and pepper. Top with cherry tomatoes if desired, and serve immediately.

Stuffed Bell Peppers

Ingredients:

- 4 bell peppers, halved and seeded
- 1 cup cooked rice (white or brown)
- 1 can (15 oz) diced tomatoes
- 1 cup black beans, rinsed and drained
- 1 tsp cumin
- 1 tsp chili powder
- 1/2 cup shredded cheese (optional)

Instructions:

Preheat the oven to 375°F (190°C). In a bowl, combine cooked rice, diced tomatoes, black beans, cumin, and chili powder. Stuff the bell pepper halves with the mixture and place them in a baking dish. If desired, top with shredded cheese. Cover with foil and bake for 25-30 minutes, then remove foil and bake for an additional 10 minutes until peppers are tender.

Vegetable Stir-Fry

Ingredients:

- 2 cups mixed vegetables (broccoli, bell peppers, carrots, snap peas)
- 2 tbsp soy sauce
- 1 tbsp sesame oil
- 2 cloves garlic, minced
- 1 tsp ginger, grated
- Cooked rice or noodles for serving

Instructions:

Heat sesame oil in a large skillet or wok over medium-high heat. Add garlic and ginger, stirring for about 30 seconds. Add mixed vegetables and stir-fry for 5-7 minutes until tender-crisp. Add soy sauce and toss to coat. Serve over cooked rice or noodles.

Brown Rice and Vegetable Pilaf

Ingredients:

- 1 cup brown rice
- 2 cups vegetable broth
- 1 cup mixed vegetables (peas, carrots, corn)
- 1 onion, diced
- 2 cloves garlic, minced
- 2 tbsp olive oil
- Salt and pepper to taste

Instructions:

In a pot, heat olive oil over medium heat. Add onion and garlic, sautéing until translucent. Stir in brown rice and toast for 1-2 minutes. Add vegetable broth and bring to a boil. Reduce to a simmer, cover, and cook for 40-45 minutes until rice is tender. Stir in mixed vegetables, season with salt and pepper, and serve warm.

Roasted Chickpeas and Sweet Potatoes

Ingredients:

- 1 can (15 oz) chickpeas, rinsed and drained
- 2 sweet potatoes, diced
- 2 tbsp olive oil
- 1 tsp paprika
- 1 tsp cumin
- Salt and pepper to taste

Instructions:

Preheat the oven to 425°F (220°C). In a bowl, toss chickpeas and sweet potatoes with olive oil, paprika, cumin, salt, and pepper. Spread on a baking sheet and roast for 25-30 minutes, stirring halfway through, until sweet potatoes are tender and chickpeas are crispy. Serve warm as a side or snack.

Spinach and Mushroom Omelet

Ingredients:

- 3 eggs
- 1 cup fresh spinach, chopped
- 1/2 cup mushrooms, sliced
- 1/4 cup cheese (optional)
- Salt and pepper to taste
- 1 tbsp olive oil

Instructions:

In a bowl, whisk the eggs with salt and pepper. Heat olive oil in a skillet over medium heat, add mushrooms, and sauté until soft. Add spinach and cook until wilted. Pour the eggs over the vegetables, cooking until the edges start to set. Sprinkle cheese on top if desired, fold the omelet, and cook for another minute until fully set. Serve warm.

Turkey and Spinach Meatballs

Ingredients:

- 1 lb ground turkey
- 1 cup fresh spinach, chopped
- 1/4 cup breadcrumbs
- 1 egg
- 2 cloves garlic, minced
- 1 tsp Italian seasoning
- Salt and pepper to taste

Instructions:

Preheat the oven to 400°F (200°C). In a bowl, combine ground turkey, spinach, breadcrumbs, egg, garlic, Italian seasoning, salt, and pepper. Form the mixture into meatballs and place on a baking sheet. Bake for 20-25 minutes until cooked through. Serve with your favorite sauce or over pasta.

Baked Tilapia with Lemon and Dill

Ingredients:

- 4 tilapia fillets
- Juice of 1 lemon
- 2 tbsp fresh dill, chopped (or 1 tbsp dried)
- 2 tbsp olive oil
- Salt and pepper to taste

Instructions:

Preheat the oven to 375°F (190°C). Place tilapia fillets on a baking dish. Drizzle with olive oil and lemon juice, then sprinkle with dill, salt, and pepper. Bake for 15-20 minutes until fish flakes easily with a fork. Serve with a side of vegetables or rice.

Cauliflower Rice Stir-Fry

Ingredients:

- 1 head cauliflower, grated or 1 package of cauliflower rice
- 2 cups mixed vegetables (carrots, peas, bell peppers)
- 2 eggs, beaten
- 2 tbsp soy sauce
- 1 tbsp sesame oil
- 2 cloves garlic, minced

Instructions:

In a large skillet, heat sesame oil over medium heat. Add garlic and sauté for 30 seconds. Add mixed vegetables and stir-fry for 3-4 minutes. Push vegetables to the side and add beaten eggs, scrambling them until cooked. Stir in cauliflower rice and soy sauce, cooking for another 5 minutes until heated through. Serve warm.

Greek Yogurt Chicken Salad

Ingredients:

- 2 cups cooked chicken, shredded
- 1/2 cup Greek yogurt
- 1/4 cup celery, diced
- 1/4 cup red onion, diced
- 1 tbsp Dijon mustard
- Salt and pepper to taste

Instructions:

In a bowl, combine shredded chicken, Greek yogurt, celery, red onion, and Dijon mustard. Mix well and season with salt and pepper. Serve on a bed of greens, in a sandwich, or as a wrap.

Vegetable Lentil Soup

Ingredients:

- 1 cup lentils, rinsed
- 4 cups vegetable broth
- 1 onion, diced
- 2 carrots, diced
- 2 celery stalks, diced
- 2 cloves garlic, minced
- 1 can (14 oz) diced tomatoes
- 1 tsp thyme
- Salt and pepper to taste

Instructions:

In a large pot, heat olive oil over medium heat. Add onion, carrots, and celery, sautéing until softened. Stir in garlic and cook for 1 minute. Add lentils, broth, diced tomatoes, thyme, salt, and pepper. Bring to a boil, then reduce heat and simmer for 30-40 minutes until lentils are tender. Serve warm.

Cabbage and Carrot Slaw

Ingredients:

- 2 cups cabbage, shredded
- 1 cup carrots, shredded
- 1/4 cup mayonnaise
- 1 tbsp apple cider vinegar
- Salt and pepper to taste

Instructions:

In a large bowl, combine shredded cabbage and carrots. In a separate bowl, whisk together mayonnaise, apple cider vinegar, salt, and pepper. Pour the dressing over the vegetables and toss to combine. Chill before serving.

Chickpea Salad with Cucumber and Tomato

Ingredients:

- 1 can (15 oz) chickpeas, rinsed and drained
- 1 cucumber, diced
- 1 cup cherry tomatoes, halved
- 1/4 red onion, diced
- 2 tbsp olive oil
- Juice of 1 lemon
- Salt and pepper to taste

Instructions:

In a large bowl, combine chickpeas, cucumber, cherry tomatoes, and red onion. Drizzle with olive oil and lemon juice, then season with salt and pepper. Toss to combine and serve chilled or at room temperature.

Grilled Vegetable Skewers

Ingredients:

- 1 zucchini, sliced
- 1 bell pepper, chopped
- 1 red onion, chopped
- 1 cup cherry tomatoes
- 2 tbsp olive oil
- 1 tsp garlic powder
- Salt and pepper to taste
- Skewers

Instructions:

Preheat the grill to medium-high heat. In a bowl, toss the vegetables with olive oil, garlic powder, salt, and pepper. Thread the vegetables onto skewers. Grill for 10-15 minutes, turning occasionally, until the vegetables are tender and slightly charred. Serve warm.

Quinoa-Stuffed Eggplant

Ingredients:

- 2 medium eggplants, halved
- 1 cup cooked quinoa
- 1 cup diced tomatoes
- 1/2 cup onion, diced
- 1/2 cup feta cheese (optional)
- 2 cloves garlic, minced
- Olive oil
- Salt and pepper to taste

Instructions:

Preheat the oven to 375°F (190°C). Scoop out the insides of the eggplant halves and set aside. In a skillet, heat olive oil and sauté onion and garlic until translucent. Add diced tomatoes, eggplant flesh, quinoa, salt, and pepper. Cook for 5 minutes. Stuff the eggplant halves with the mixture, top with feta cheese if desired, and bake for 25-30 minutes. Serve hot.

Chicken and Vegetable Stir-Fry

Ingredients:

- 1 lb chicken breast, sliced
- 2 cups mixed vegetables (bell peppers, broccoli, carrots)
- 2 tbsp soy sauce
- 1 tbsp sesame oil
- 2 cloves garlic, minced
- 1 tsp ginger, minced
- Cooked rice for serving

Instructions:

In a large skillet, heat sesame oil over medium-high heat. Add chicken and cook until browned. Add garlic, ginger, and mixed vegetables, stirring for 5-7 minutes until the vegetables are tender. Pour in soy sauce and cook for another minute. Serve over cooked rice.

Baked Sweet Potatoes with Black Beans

Ingredients:

- 4 medium sweet potatoes
- 1 can (15 oz) black beans, rinsed and drained
- 1 tsp cumin
- 1 tsp chili powder
- Salt and pepper to taste
- Toppings: avocado, salsa, cilantro (optional)

Instructions:

Preheat the oven to 400°F (200°C). Pierce sweet potatoes with a fork and bake for 45-60 minutes until tender. In a bowl, mix black beans with cumin, chili powder, salt, and pepper. Once sweet potatoes are done, slice them open and fill with the black bean mixture. Top with avocado, salsa, and cilantro if desired.

Veggie-Packed Frittata

Ingredients:

- 6 eggs
- 1 cup spinach, chopped
- 1/2 cup bell pepper, diced
- 1/2 cup mushrooms, sliced
- 1/4 cup cheese (optional)
- Salt and pepper to taste
- Olive oil

Instructions:

Preheat the oven to 350°F (175°C). In a bowl, whisk the eggs with salt and pepper. In a skillet, heat olive oil and sauté bell pepper and mushrooms until softened. Add spinach and cook until wilted. Pour the eggs over the vegetables, cook for 2 minutes, then transfer to the oven. Bake for 15-20 minutes until set. Top with cheese if desired before serving.

Broccoli and Cauliflower Salad

Ingredients:

- 2 cups broccoli florets
- 2 cups cauliflower florets
- 1/2 cup red onion, diced
- 1/4 cup raisins or cranberries
- 1/4 cup sunflower seeds
- 1/2 cup Greek yogurt or mayonnaise
- 1 tbsp apple cider vinegar
- Salt and pepper to taste

Instructions:

In a large bowl, combine broccoli, cauliflower, red onion, raisins, and sunflower seeds. In a separate bowl, mix Greek yogurt (or mayonnaise), apple cider vinegar, salt, and pepper. Pour the dressing over the salad and toss to combine. Chill before serving.

Turkey and Vegetable Lettuce Wraps

Ingredients:

- 1 lb ground turkey
- 1 cup bell pepper, diced
- 1/2 cup carrots, shredded
- 2 cloves garlic, minced
- 2 tbsp soy sauce
- Lettuce leaves (iceberg or romaine)

Instructions:

In a skillet, cook ground turkey over medium heat until browned. Add bell pepper, carrots, and garlic, cooking for another 5 minutes. Stir in soy sauce and cook for 2 more minutes. Spoon the turkey mixture into lettuce leaves and serve as wraps.

Roasted Beet and Arugula Salad

Ingredients:

- 2 medium beets, roasted and sliced
- 4 cups arugula
- 1/4 cup goat cheese, crumbled
- 1/4 cup walnuts, toasted
- 2 tbsp balsamic vinegar
- 2 tbsp olive oil
- Salt and pepper to taste

Instructions:

In a large bowl, combine arugula, roasted beets, goat cheese, and walnuts. In a small bowl, whisk together balsamic vinegar, olive oil, salt, and pepper. Drizzle the dressing over the salad and toss gently to combine. Serve immediately.

Sautéed Kale with Garlic

Ingredients:

- 1 bunch kale, stems removed and chopped
- 2 cloves garlic, minced
- 1 tbsp olive oil
- Salt and pepper to taste

Instructions:

In a large skillet, heat olive oil over medium heat. Add garlic and sauté for 30 seconds. Add chopped kale, cooking for 5-7 minutes until wilted. Season with salt and pepper before serving.

Mediterranean Couscous Salad

Ingredients:

- 1 cup couscous
- 1 1/4 cups vegetable broth
- 1 cup cherry tomatoes, halved
- 1 cucumber, diced
- 1/2 red onion, diced
- 1/2 cup kalamata olives, sliced
- 1/2 cup feta cheese, crumbled
- 1/4 cup fresh parsley, chopped
- 3 tbsp olive oil
- 2 tbsp lemon juice
- Salt and pepper to taste

Instructions:

In a saucepan, bring the vegetable broth to a boil. Stir in the couscous, cover, and remove from heat. Let it sit for 5 minutes, then fluff with a fork. In a large bowl, combine the couscous, cherry tomatoes, cucumber, red onion, olives, feta cheese, and parsley. Drizzle with olive oil and lemon juice, then season with salt and pepper. Toss to combine and serve chilled or at room temperature.

Stuffed Zucchini Boats

Ingredients:

- 4 medium zucchinis, halved lengthwise
- 1 cup cooked quinoa
- 1 cup marinara sauce
- 1/2 cup mozzarella cheese, shredded
- 1/4 cup grated Parmesan cheese
- 1/2 tsp Italian seasoning
- Salt and pepper to taste

Instructions:

Preheat the oven to 375°F (190°C). Scoop out the insides of the zucchini halves and chop the flesh. In a bowl, mix cooked quinoa, chopped zucchini, marinara sauce, mozzarella cheese, Parmesan cheese, Italian seasoning, salt, and pepper. Stuff the zucchini halves with the mixture and place them in a baking dish. Bake for 25-30 minutes until the zucchini is tender and the tops are golden.

Lentil and Vegetable Stew

Ingredients:

- 1 cup lentils, rinsed
- 1 onion, chopped
- 2 carrots, diced
- 2 celery stalks, diced
- 2 cloves garlic, minced
- 4 cups vegetable broth
- 1 can (14 oz) diced tomatoes
- 1 tsp cumin
- 1 tsp thyme
- Salt and pepper to taste

Instructions:

In a large pot, sauté onion, carrots, and celery over medium heat until softened. Add garlic and cook for another minute. Stir in lentils, vegetable broth, diced tomatoes, cumin, thyme, salt, and pepper. Bring to a boil, then reduce heat and simmer for 30-35 minutes until lentils are tender. Serve hot.

Oven-Baked Chicken with Herbs

Ingredients:

- 4 chicken breasts
- 2 tbsp olive oil
- 2 tsp dried rosemary
- 2 tsp dried thyme
- 1 tsp garlic powder
- Salt and pepper to taste

Instructions:

Preheat the oven to 400°F (200°C). In a bowl, mix olive oil, rosemary, thyme, garlic powder, salt, and pepper. Rub the mixture over the chicken breasts and place them in a baking dish. Bake for 25-30 minutes or until the chicken is cooked through and juices run clear. Serve with your choice of sides.

Fresh Tomato and Basil Pasta

Ingredients:

- 8 oz pasta of choice
- 4 ripe tomatoes, diced
- 1/4 cup fresh basil, chopped
- 2 cloves garlic, minced
- 3 tbsp olive oil
- Salt and pepper to taste
- Grated Parmesan cheese for serving

Instructions:

Cook pasta according to package instructions. In a large bowl, combine diced tomatoes, basil, garlic, olive oil, salt, and pepper. Once the pasta is cooked, drain and toss it with the tomato mixture. Serve topped with grated Parmesan cheese.

Grilled Shrimp Tacos with Cabbage Slaw

Ingredients:

- 1 lb shrimp, peeled and deveined
- 1 tbsp olive oil
- 1 tsp chili powder
- 1/2 tsp cumin
- Salt and pepper to taste
- 8 corn tortillas
- 2 cups cabbage, shredded
- 1/4 cup cilantro, chopped
- 1 lime, juiced

Instructions:

In a bowl, toss shrimp with olive oil, chili powder, cumin, salt, and pepper. Grill the shrimp for 2-3 minutes per side until cooked through. In another bowl, mix cabbage, cilantro, and lime juice. To assemble tacos, place grilled shrimp in tortillas and top with cabbage slaw. Serve immediately.

Eggplant Parmesan (Low-Sodium)

Ingredients:

- 2 medium eggplants, sliced
- 1 cup whole wheat breadcrumbs
- 2 cups marinara sauce
- 1/2 cup mozzarella cheese, shredded
- 1/4 cup grated Parmesan cheese
- 1/4 cup fresh basil, chopped
- Olive oil spray

Instructions:

Preheat the oven to 375°F (190°C). Sprinkle eggplant slices with salt and let them sit for 30 minutes to draw out moisture. Rinse and pat dry. Spray a baking sheet with olive oil and arrange eggplant slices in a single layer. Bake for 20 minutes, flipping halfway. In a baking dish, layer marinara sauce, eggplant, breadcrumbs, mozzarella, and Parmesan. Repeat layers and top with basil. Bake for 30-35 minutes until bubbly.

Roasted Vegetable Medley

Ingredients:

- 2 cups mixed vegetables (carrots, bell peppers, zucchini, and broccoli)
- 2 tbsp olive oil
- 1 tsp garlic powder
- 1 tsp Italian seasoning
- Salt and pepper to taste

Instructions:

Preheat the oven to 425°F (220°C). In a large bowl, toss the mixed vegetables with olive oil, garlic powder, Italian seasoning, salt, and pepper. Spread the vegetables on a baking sheet in a single layer. Roast for 25-30 minutes until tender and slightly caramelized, stirring halfway through.

Wild Rice and Cranberry Salad

Ingredients:

- 1 cup wild rice, cooked
- 1/2 cup dried cranberries
- 1/2 cup pecans, chopped
- 1/4 cup green onions, sliced
- 1/4 cup parsley, chopped
- 3 tbsp olive oil
- 2 tbsp apple cider vinegar
- Salt and pepper to taste

Instructions:

In a large bowl, combine cooked wild rice, cranberries, pecans, green onions, and parsley. In a small bowl, whisk together olive oil, apple cider vinegar, salt, and pepper. Drizzle the dressing over the salad and toss to combine. Serve chilled or at room temperature.

Spaghetti Squash with Marinara

Ingredients:

- 1 medium spaghetti squash
- 2 cups marinara sauce
- 1/2 cup grated Parmesan cheese
- 1/4 cup fresh basil, chopped
- Salt and pepper to taste
- Olive oil

Instructions:

1. Preheat the oven to 400°F (200°C). Cut the spaghetti squash in half lengthwise and scoop out the seeds. Drizzle with olive oil, and season with salt and pepper.
2. Place the squash cut-side down on a baking sheet and bake for 30-40 minutes until tender.
3. In a saucepan, heat the marinara sauce over medium heat.
4. Once the squash is cooked, use a fork to scrape out the strands into a bowl.
5. Combine the spaghetti squash with marinara sauce, and top with Parmesan cheese and fresh basil. Serve warm.

Chicken Quinoa Bowl

Ingredients:

- 1 cup cooked quinoa
- 1 cup cooked chicken, shredded
- 1 cup mixed vegetables (bell peppers, carrots, and broccoli)
- 1/4 cup hummus or tahini
- 1 tbsp olive oil
- Salt and pepper to taste

Instructions:

1. In a skillet, heat olive oil over medium heat. Add mixed vegetables and sauté until tender.
2. In a large bowl, combine cooked quinoa, shredded chicken, and sautéed vegetables.
3. Add hummus or tahini, and season with salt and pepper. Toss to combine.
4. Serve warm, garnished with additional hummus or tahini if desired.

Asian Cabbage Salad

Ingredients:

- 4 cups shredded cabbage
- 1 cup shredded carrots
- 1/2 cup green onions, chopped
- 1/2 cup almonds or sesame seeds
- 1/4 cup cilantro, chopped

Dressing:

- 1/4 cup soy sauce
- 2 tbsp rice vinegar
- 2 tbsp sesame oil
- 1 tbsp honey
- 1 tsp grated ginger

Instructions:

1. In a large bowl, combine shredded cabbage, carrots, green onions, almonds or sesame seeds, and cilantro.
2. In a separate bowl, whisk together soy sauce, rice vinegar, sesame oil, honey, and grated ginger.
3. Pour the dressing over the salad and toss to coat. Serve immediately or refrigerate for 30 minutes to allow flavors to meld.

Lemon Garlic Shrimp and Broccoli

Ingredients:

- 1 lb shrimp, peeled and deveined
- 2 cups broccoli florets
- 4 cloves garlic, minced
- 2 tbsp olive oil
- Juice of 1 lemon
- Salt and pepper to taste

Instructions:

1. In a large skillet, heat olive oil over medium heat. Add minced garlic and sauté for 1 minute until fragrant.
2. Add broccoli florets and cook for 3-4 minutes until bright green and tender.
3. Add shrimp, lemon juice, salt, and pepper. Cook for another 3-5 minutes until shrimp are cooked through.
4. Serve immediately, garnished with lemon wedges if desired.

Baked Portobello Mushrooms

Ingredients:

- 4 large portobello mushrooms
- 2 tbsp balsamic vinegar
- 2 tbsp olive oil
- 1 tsp garlic powder
- 1/2 cup mozzarella cheese, shredded
- Salt and pepper to taste

Instructions:

1. Preheat the oven to 375°F (190°C).
2. In a small bowl, mix balsamic vinegar, olive oil, garlic powder, salt, and pepper.
3. Brush the mixture onto both sides of the portobello mushrooms and place them on a baking sheet.
4. Bake for 15-20 minutes until tender. Remove from the oven, sprinkle with mozzarella cheese, and bake for an additional 5 minutes until cheese is melted. Serve warm.

Avocado and Tomato Salad

Ingredients:

- 2 ripe avocados, diced
- 2 cups cherry tomatoes, halved
- 1/4 cup red onion, finely chopped
- 2 tbsp olive oil
- Juice of 1 lime
- Salt and pepper to taste
- Fresh cilantro or basil for garnish

Instructions:

1. In a large bowl, combine diced avocados, cherry tomatoes, and red onion.
2. Drizzle with olive oil and lime juice, then season with salt and pepper.
3. Gently toss to combine, being careful not to mash the avocados.
4. Garnish with fresh cilantro or basil before serving.

Vegetable and Bean Chili

Ingredients:

- 1 can (15 oz) black beans, drained and rinsed
- 1 can (15 oz) kidney beans, drained and rinsed
- 1 can (14 oz) diced tomatoes
- 1 bell pepper, diced
- 1 onion, chopped
- 2 cloves garlic, minced
- 1 tbsp chili powder
- 1 tsp cumin
- Salt and pepper to taste
- 1 cup vegetable broth

Instructions:

1. In a large pot, sauté onion, bell pepper, and garlic until softened.
2. Add black beans, kidney beans, diced tomatoes, vegetable broth, chili powder, cumin, salt, and pepper.
3. Bring to a boil, then reduce heat and simmer for 20-30 minutes.
4. Serve hot, garnished with fresh cilantro or avocado if desired.

Savory Oatmeal with Spinach

Ingredients:

- 1 cup rolled oats
- 2 cups vegetable broth or water
- 2 cups fresh spinach
- 1/4 cup grated Parmesan cheese
- Salt and pepper to taste
- 1 egg (optional)

Instructions:

1. In a saucepan, bring vegetable broth or water to a boil. Stir in rolled oats and reduce heat to simmer for 5 minutes until creamy.
2. Stir in fresh spinach and cook until wilted.
3. Season with salt and pepper and top with grated Parmesan cheese. For a more filling dish, you can poach or fry an egg and place it on top before serving.

Grilled Turkey Burgers

Ingredients:

- 1 lb ground turkey
- 1/4 cup breadcrumbs
- 1/4 cup grated Parmesan cheese
- 1 clove garlic, minced
- 1 tsp Italian seasoning
- Salt and pepper to taste
- Whole wheat burger buns

Instructions:

1. Preheat the grill to medium-high heat.
2. In a bowl, combine ground turkey, breadcrumbs, Parmesan cheese, garlic, Italian seasoning, salt, and pepper.
3. Form the mixture into burger patties.
4. Grill for 5-7 minutes on each side, or until cooked through. Serve on whole wheat buns with your choice of toppings.

Roasted Brussels Sprouts with Almonds

Ingredients:

- 1 lb Brussels sprouts, halved
- 1/2 cup sliced almonds
- 3 tbsp olive oil
- Salt and pepper to taste
- 1/4 cup balsamic vinegar (optional)

Instructions:

1. Preheat the oven to 400°F (200°C).
2. In a large bowl, toss the halved Brussels sprouts with olive oil, salt, and pepper.
3. Spread the Brussels sprouts on a baking sheet in a single layer.
4. Roast for 20-25 minutes until crispy and golden, stirring halfway through.
5. In the last 5 minutes of roasting, sprinkle sliced almonds over the Brussels sprouts and return to the oven.
6. Drizzle with balsamic vinegar before serving if desired.

Sweet Potato and Black Bean Tacos

Ingredients:

- 2 medium sweet potatoes, peeled and diced
- 1 can (15 oz) black beans, drained and rinsed
- 1 tsp cumin
- 1 tsp chili powder
- Salt and pepper to taste
- Corn or flour tortillas
- Toppings: avocado, salsa, cilantro, lime wedges

Instructions:

1. Preheat the oven to 425°F (220°C). Toss diced sweet potatoes with olive oil, cumin, chili powder, salt, and pepper.
2. Spread on a baking sheet and roast for 25-30 minutes until tender and caramelized.
3. In a small saucepan, heat black beans until warm.
4. To assemble, place roasted sweet potatoes and black beans in tortillas and top with your choice of toppings. Serve immediately.

Ratatouille

Ingredients:

- 1 eggplant, diced
- 2 zucchini, sliced
- 1 bell pepper, chopped
- 1 onion, chopped
- 2 cups diced tomatoes (canned or fresh)
- 3 cloves garlic, minced
- 2 tbsp olive oil
- 1 tsp dried thyme
- Salt and pepper to taste
- Fresh basil for garnish

Instructions:

1. In a large pot, heat olive oil over medium heat. Add onion and garlic, sautéing until softened.
2. Add eggplant and bell pepper, cooking until softened (about 5 minutes).
3. Stir in zucchini, diced tomatoes, thyme, salt, and pepper. Simmer for 20-30 minutes, stirring occasionally.
4. Garnish with fresh basil before serving, and serve hot as a main or side dish.

Butternut Squash Soup

Ingredients:

- 1 medium butternut squash, peeled and diced
- 1 onion, chopped
- 3 cloves garlic, minced
- 4 cups vegetable broth
- 1 tsp ground ginger
- 1/2 cup coconut milk
- Salt and pepper to taste

Instructions:

1. In a large pot, sauté onion and garlic in olive oil until softened.
2. Add diced butternut squash, vegetable broth, ground ginger, salt, and pepper. Bring to a boil.
3. Reduce heat and simmer for 20-25 minutes until squash is tender.
4. Use an immersion blender to purée the soup until smooth. Stir in coconut milk and heat through. Serve warm.

Thai Coconut Curry with Vegetables

Ingredients:

- 1 can (14 oz) coconut milk
- 2 cups mixed vegetables (bell peppers, carrots, broccoli)
- 1 tbsp red curry paste
- 1 tbsp soy sauce
- 1 tsp lime juice
- Fresh cilantro for garnish

Instructions:

1. In a large skillet, heat coconut milk over medium heat. Stir in red curry paste until combined.
2. Add mixed vegetables and cook for 5-7 minutes until tender.
3. Stir in soy sauce and lime juice.
4. Serve hot, garnished with fresh cilantro over rice or noodles if desired.

Spinach and Feta Stuffed Chicken Breast

Ingredients:

- 4 boneless, skinless chicken breasts
- 2 cups fresh spinach, chopped
- 1/2 cup feta cheese, crumbled
- 1/4 cup cream cheese, softened
- 2 tbsp olive oil
- Salt and pepper to taste

Instructions:

1. Preheat the oven to 375°F (190°C).
2. In a bowl, mix chopped spinach, feta cheese, and cream cheese.
3. Cut a pocket into each chicken breast and stuff with the spinach mixture. Secure with toothpicks if needed.
4. Season the chicken with olive oil, salt, and pepper, then place in a baking dish.
5. Bake for 25-30 minutes until cooked through. Serve hot.

Brown Rice Sushi Rolls

Ingredients:

- 2 cups cooked brown rice
- 4 sheets nori (seaweed)
- 1 cucumber, julienned
- 1 carrot, julienned
- 1 avocado, sliced
- Soy sauce for dipping

Instructions:

1. Lay a sheet of nori on a bamboo sushi mat or clean surface.
2. Spread 1/2 cup of cooked brown rice evenly over the nori, leaving a 1-inch border at the top.
3. Layer cucumber, carrot, and avocado along the bottom edge of the rice.
4. Roll the sushi tightly away from you, using the mat to help shape it. Moisten the top edge of the nori to seal the roll.
5. Slice the roll into bite-sized pieces and serve with soy sauce for dipping.